T0277111

Work
Well in
Groups

Sara Miller McCune founded SAGE Publishing in 1965 to support the dissemination of usable knowledge and educate a global community. SAGE publishes more than 1000 journals and over 800 new books each year, spanning a wide range of subject areas. Our growing selection of library products includes archives, data, case studies and video. SAGE remains majority owned by our founder and after her lifetime will become owned by a charitable trust that secures the company's continued independence.

Los Angeles | London | New Delhi | Singapore | Washington DC | Melbourne

SUPER
QUICK
SKILLS

Work
Well in
Groups

Diana Hopkins
Tom Reid

Los Angeles | London | New Delhi
Singapore | Washington DC | Melbourne

Los Angeles | London | New Delhi
Singapore | Washington DC | Melbourne

SAGE Publications Ltd
1 Oliver's Yard
55 City Road
London EC1Y 1SP

SAGE Publications Inc.
2455 Teller Road
Thousand Oaks, California 91320

SAGE Publications India Pvt Ltd
B 1/I 1 Mohan Cooperative Industrial Area
Mathura Road
New Delhi 110 044

SAGE Publications Asia-Pacific Pte Ltd
3 Church Street
#10-04 Samsung Hub
Singapore 049483

Editor: Jai Seaman
Editorial assistant: Lauren Jacobs
Production editor: Nicola Carrier
Proofreader: Sharon Cawood
Marketing manager: Catherine Slinn
Cover design: Shaun Mercier
Typeset by: C&M Digitals (P) Ltd, Chennai, India
Printed in the UK

Library of Congress Control Number: 2019955164

British Library Cataloguing in Publication data

A catalogue record for this book is available
from the British Library

ISBN 978-1-5297-1897-3

Contents

Everything in this book!

Why am I being asked to work in a group?

10 second summary

Find out what your tutor expects you to do and why, and what different types of group working there are.

Why is group working important?

Having experience and practice of working with other people who may have different ways of doing things from you is not only useful at university. It is also a prized employability skill. It's a great chance to develop your communication skills and learn more about yourself.

Group work at university allows you to:

- Learn more about the academic topic (by learning from and communicating to your peers)

- Produce a sophisticated product through pooling resources, ideas and approaches

- Build confidence by sharing responsibility

- Build awareness of how personal responsibility to the group leads to better teamwork

- Recognise that individual success can be dependent on teamwork

- Learn more about yourself and others

- Value **diversity** and **inclusivity**

- Understand different communication styles and personality types

- Develop transferable professional skills and enhance your **employability** prospects.

Diversity
the different types of people that may make up groups (in terms of nationality, race, religion, gender, age, disability etc).

Inclusivity
the practice or policy of including many different types of people, who may otherwise be excluded, and treating them with fairness and equity.

Employability
the attributes of a person that enable them to gain and maintain employment.

What types of group working are there?

There are several different kinds of things you may be asked to do as a group:

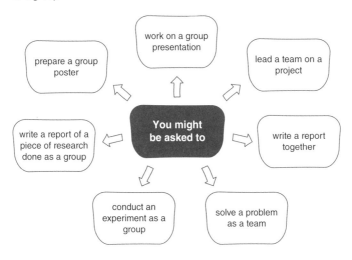

What is your tutor looking for?

Your tutor wants to see that you can demonstrate the following skills:

- Interpersonal/intercultural communication

- Problem solving and negotiation

- Decision making

- Leadership

- Conflict resolution

- **Time management**

- Oral, visual and/or written communication.

Time management
the process of
organising and using
time effectively to
improve productivity.

What types of assessment should I expect?

Your tutor may give you an individual mark for your contribution to the group assessment; they may give your group a single mark; or there may be a mixture of both. In each **scenario**, there are a few things to consider:

1   Individual marks awarded for your contribution only.

This assessment method may seem the easiest to manage. You might think you only have yourself to worry about. However, tutors will be looking for an effective inter-group dynamic, and individual marks may be influenced by how well this is demonstrated.

2   A single group mark may be awarded and based on whole group performance, and individual performances contribute to the whole group mark.

In this scenario, there is pressure is on every group member to perform well, and this can have both positive and negative effects on group dynamics, cooperation and performance. A group score can focus minds and improve motivation. However, if one or more member is struggling or not contributing, this can lead to group **conflict**.

3   In a combined assessment, separate individual scores may be presented alongside a whole group mark, and the total is then averaged.

In this type of assessment method, the pressure is on both individual members and the whole group to perform well.

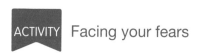

ACTIVITY Facing your fears

Answer these questions to find ways to confront your anxiety around group work.

What are your greatest fears about working in groups?

....

....

....

....

What can you do to reduce your concerns?

....

....

....

....

A student told us

'I'm worried about who I'll be working with. Do I get to choose?'

The way you are put into groups can vary. It may be your tutor who decides, or you may decide for yourselves.

Who decides?	What happens?	Strengths and challenges

Tutor decides	Group allocation may be:
	
	• random
	• based on criteria such as:
	  o demographics (e.g. previous experience; gender; nationality)
	  o research interests
	  o size of the class
	  o personality types
		Being allocated your group by your tutor may:
		
		• provide the group with a wide and dynamic skills and experience pool
		• create a dynamic skill set within the group
		
		Be aware, however, that it may also:
		
		• require 'getting to know each other' time
		• need effort to ensure you 'gel' as a team

You decide	You choose the people you want to work with. This usually means you choose your friends rather than random classmates!	Working with your friends may have the following advantages: • you understand each other's personalities and communication styles • you don't need time to get to know each other Be aware, however, that you may also: • be a bit too relaxed and not work as effectively • find out that working together is very different from friendship • find differences of opinion/conflict complicated and difficult to resolve

'Coming together is a beginning, staying together is progress, and working together is success.'

Henry Ford

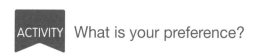

ACTIVITY What is your preference?

Consider the following questions:

1   Would you prefer to form your own group or be allocated your group by your tutor? Why?

....

....

....

....

2   What kind of assessment do you like most? Why?

....

....

....

....

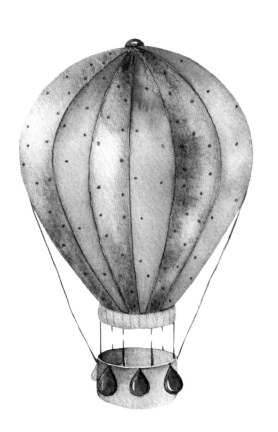

What should I do first?

10 second summary

You will find out that getting to know your team at the outset is the most important factor in successful group working.

60 second summary

First impressions count

There is a temptation for newly formed groups to jump straight into the task. However, before you think about what your tutor has asked you to do and the details of the assignment, you need to spend some time getting to know each other; your interests, strengths and preferences when it comes to dividing up the work. For example, you may discover that one member is keen on writing or editing, while another may be a whizz on PowerPoint and other visuals. Getting to know each other will also help you ensure that members are doing tasks that suit their skill set. You may also learn a little of each other's learning styles and personalities.

A student told us

'I don't know how to prepare for group working.'

Get set for group work

Before you start your group-working task, it is important to understand how groups function. One of the best ways to do this is to look at Bruce Tuckman's four-stage **group development theory or model** (Forming, Storming, Norming, Performing).

Tuckman's model shows how new groups often progress through four stages when working on a task.

Group development theory (Forming, Storming, Norming, Performing) Bruce Tuckman's theory sets out the process a group goes through when it works on a task, from the initial formation stage, through facing challenges, dealing with and solving problems, to finally working effectively to complete the project.

Forming	Storming	Norming	Performing

In this initial stage, group members are likely to be polite and formal. Some members may be anxious while others are excited by the challenge. Orientation is key to the success of the group. If you neglect it, then trouble can lie ahead, such as misunderstand-ings, conflict, poor performance, people assigned to the wrong tasks or roles, and so on.

Successful group forming establishes group identity and unity from the start, and a culture of respect, honesty and support.

Once you start your project, you and your fellow group members may face challenges as you discover different approaches to working, different ideas, personality clashes, and so on. There might be flashpoints (for example, if the first deadline is not met).

This is a normal part of the group working process, and if you have set up your group effectively, with a clear set of ground rules, etc. (see Section 5), then you should be able to resolve conflict and issues quickly before they escalate.

At this stage, conflicts are resolved and the group starts to find a way to work well together. You have developed a good understanding of each other's approaches and personalities and everyone has settled into their roles.

In the fourth stage, the group successfully completes the tasks set.

Tip!

It may be useful to talk about Tuckman's model during the forming stage, and refer back to it when necessary, particularly if disagreement or conflict arises.

Following Tuckman's model, the first thing your group needs to do is get to know each other; find out about each other's strengths, likes and dislikes, and any concerns you may have about the group task. This will help your group:

- Assign the right people to the right role

- Develop group unity and identity

- Foster openness and honesty

- Reduce the risk of conflict further down the line.

'Getting to know you' topics

Group familiarisation topics (before you get into discussing the task itself) might include:

Backgrounds

Talk about your routes to your course subjects taken, choices made, wins and hurdles along the way.

Impressions of the course so far

Talk about the course and what you like and don't like – and why.

Likes and dislikes

Talk about the types of tasks you like to do, and those you don't like – e.g. 'I'm a good writer' or 'I really struggle with time management'. If you can be as honest with each other as possible, it will save you a lot of grief further down the line.

Roles

Talk about roles you feel comfortable with, such as leader, time keeper, researcher, editor, secretary, and so on. What roles would you find challenging? One of the keys to being a successful team player is being prepared to try things that are outside of your comfort zone. Group learning is a journey of self-discovery.

How you feel about group working

Talk about why you feel confident or nervous about group working. What are your concerns and worries? This is probably the most difficult topic to discuss as it requires a level of honesty and trust that may not be present within the group yet. However, if you air your concerns at the start of the project, you are likely to reach an effective team dynamic more quickly.

Getting to know the task

Once you've spent some time introducing yourselves to each other, you can then move on to getting to know the task.

Here you should look together at all of the information your tutor has provided; assessment type, task instructions, mark scheme, rules, etc. At this stage you might:

- Check understanding of the task and clarify any grey areas

- Identify any anticipated problems

- Make a list of questions to ask the tutor (if you can't answer them yourselves)

- Consider the challenges of the task type – e.g. How do we deal with a group presentation or group written report?

- Consider roles and who does what (see Section 3)

- Start to think about timescales and workloads – How can the project be divided into manageable chunks of work? (see Section 4)

- Establish a set of ground rules that you all should follow (see Section 5).

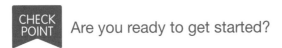

CHECK POINT Are you ready to get started?

Why is it important to get to know your team mates when you first form a group?

....

....

....

....

How do you know what your tutor wants you to do?

....

....

....

....

What does Tuckman's model tell you about group working?

....

....

....

....

How does my group decide who does what?

10 second summary

You will get advice on how to identify strengths and personal preferences in your group and set roles accordingly.

60 second summary

The roles of engagement

Once you have successfully navigated your introductions and orientated yourselves with your project or assignment, the next task is to establish who does what. You should have already talked about each other's skills, strengths and weaknesses, and preferences, and now you need to nail down the specific roles of each team member, based on your discussions. There are a number of key roles that you should consider including, as these may be vital in the effectiveness of your group performance. But it is important to be open-minded and ready to compromise, and to work together in the interests of the team as a whole. Remember, group working is an opportunity to develop new skills.

In order to ensure your group works efficiently and effectively, you need to be able to take advantage of the skills pool available within your team and assign the most suitable roles to each individual. Choosing the right person for the right job can make or break the success of group working, so it is vital you choose wisely.

Play your role to reach your goal!

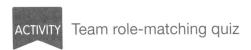

ACTIVITY Team role-matching quiz

Look at the list of group roles on the following pages and the corresponding skills profile, and ask yourself the following questions:

Which role do you identify with most?

Do you have the right qualifications for the job?

Role	Skills Profile
Group leader/co-ordinator The group leader may be responsible for: • enforcing group rules • ensuring group cohesion • ensuring targets are met • ensuring that everyone is contributing equally to the group • final decisions and signing off your group project • ensuring group cohesion, and acting as mediator/referee in disputes and arguments The level of power your leader has should be agreed by the group. You might keep the same group leader throughout the project or rotate responsibilities.	Well-organised Level-headed Confident Honest Fair Inspires and motivates Good communicator Committed to the project Decision-maker Diplomatic Decisive Supportive Problem-solver Innovator Practical Empathiser
The chairperson: • ensures meetings run smoothly and to time • ensures everyone has a voice and discussions don't escalate into conflict • summarises decisions taken and sets the agenda for the next meeting You might choose to nominate one person for this role or rotate during your project. This role is more referee and less managerial.	Well-organised Good time keeper Good communicator Approachable Non-judgemental Understands the big picture Team player Thorough and accurate record-keeper Good negotiator Decision-maker Motivator Moderator

The editor:	Understands the project brief
 • collects and collates project materials from group members, for example different sections of a report, presentation slides • ensures a unified style and approach, and that individual contributions link together • identifies any issues or gaps; checks length and edits if necessary • proofreads the final work, checking for spelling and grammar mistakes	Understands the audience and style required
	Well-organised
	Accurate and thorough
	Confident negotiator/ decision-maker
	Good communicator – you will need to explain editorial options and decisions
	Good time-keeper and deadline achiever
	Can work under pressure
	Non-judgemental
	Expert in the project medium (writing, presentations, etc.)
The researcher:	Well-organised/systematic
 • investigates and finds relevant and suitable materials (background information, academic texts, examples and case studies, statistics and any other evidence to support the project) • collects and collates information and sources and disseminates to the group	Expert in library catalogue, databases and online research
	Accurate and effective note-taking and summary skills
	Ability to scope from big picture to detail; to identify and filter relevant topics/sub-topics
	A curious mind
	Ability to find links between sources and gaps in thinking
	Critical thinking skills (analysis and evaluation of sources)
The administrator:	Well-organised and efficient
 • maintains accurate records of meetings: agendas, minutes, actions and decisions, etc. • communicates all important information to the group	Deadline-driven, time-keeper
	Good IT skills
	Good communicator – verbal and written
	Strategic thinker

A student told us

'I never knew I was good at leading a team until I tried it.'

Use the table above to think carefully about which role is most suitable for you and decide together, as a team, who does what.

You might find that you have more than one person who is suitable for a particular role. That's great! You are already winning! In this case, you could rotate the role, or share responsibilities. BUT you will have to work out beforehand how you are going to work together to ensure a unified approach.

You might also decide that a leader role is unnecessary. This may be okay too, as long as your group is confident that you have the drive, focus and commitment to complete the assignment without a leader to help steer your project to completion.

Role switch and review

During the early planning stages of your group project, you might agree to set a date for a rotation of some or all of the roles. The advantage of this is that a change of roles can bring fresh ideas and momentum, and it can also resolve any issues the group may be experiencing with a particular individual and their designated role.

You may, of course, agree to continue with the same roles, as everything is running smoothly, but at least you have the option to switch in place, just in case things aren't quite working out.

If you do decide to switch roles, this should always be a group decision, to avoid or reduce disagreements.

Do you know how to make roles work in a group?

What are the advantages of assigning roles for group work?

....

....

....

....

Why is it important to match the right person with the most suitable role?

....

....

....

....

What do you do if the role isn't right for you?

....

....

....

....

Congratulations

You've introduced yourselves, got to know each other's strengths, and set roles and responsibilities within your group. Now … the hard work begins.

How can I become a good team member?

10 second
summary

Here you will find out how to improve
your interpersonal communication
skills to help you work effectively in a
group environment.

All for one and one for all

Being an effective team member is primarily about being an effective communicator, but it is, of course, more than that. The success of any team is dependent on each of you having a clear understanding of your role, what you are supposed to do, and how you can support, encourage and motivate one another, and contribute to the team's identity and goals. Alongside this, you will enhance your team cooperation and unity by developing an insight and understanding of individual behaviour types, including your own, and responding effectively to these different approaches and responses. If you are working in an international learning context, then intercultural awareness can also enhance group performance and minimise misunderstandings and disagreements.

A successful team is made up of successful team players. Great team players show commitment, encourage and inspire, and are always ready to help and support their colleagues.

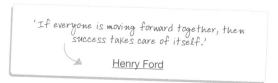

'If everyone is moving forward together, then success takes care of itself.'

Henry Ford

What makes an ideal team player?

An ideal **team player** is:

- **Reliable and dependent**

  You can be relied upon to meet deadlines, be prepared for and attend meetings, and produce high quality work and deliver on time.

- **A confident communicator**

  You can articulate ideas and express your views clearly. You also need to be a good listener, give your team mates time to communicate their ideas, and respond to them constructively in a calm, measured and reasoned manner.

- **Open-minded and flexible**

  You should be open-minded and avoid being too dogmatic. You should be ready and willing to switch roles and/or change direction for the good of the group and the project.

- **Committed**

  You should be fully behind the project, helping to drive it forward. You should also demonstrate your enthusiasm for and loyalty to your team, supporting and encouraging others and boosting team morale.

- **Reflective**

  You need to understand your own actions and behaviour, through **reflection**, as this will help you understand the behaviour of others. A good team player reflects on how they are performing and communicating in the group, and considers ways to improve, modify or adapt their behaviour and/or communication to fit the group dynamic.

  > Reflection a process of thinking deeply about past activities, feelings and behaviours in order to develop skills and enhance future performance.

- **Cooperative**

  A good team player is cooperative rather than competitive. You should be willing to compromise and concede in arguments, accept the views of others and be prepared to change your mind.

- **Solution-focused**

  You should be actively seeking solutions to problems rather than getting bogged down and complaining about problems.

- **Supportive**

  If a team member is struggling with their part of the project, a good team player will offer to help resolve the particular issue they are having and, if necessary, share some of the burden.

- **Level-headed**

  When the pressure is on, deadlines are tight and/or problems arise, good team players remain calm, level-headed and solution-focused.

- **Prepared to go the extra mile**

  You should be willing to step up and take on additional work, if necessary.

'I prefer to work alone, but I know group working skills are valuable skills to have. What should I do to become a better team player?'

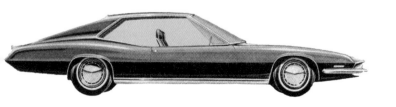

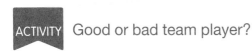
Good or bad team player?

Imagine your group task is to design an activity to teach secondary school children about an area of research being done at your university. In your group, you have agreed different tasks.

Which of the following descriptions would make the best team player?

A   One of your group likes to work alone, doesn't like discussing their ideas or work, and has stopped communicating with the other group members completely. On the day that you have planned to meet to discuss the final product, this group member presents what they have done. Their work is thorough and complete, but because of the lack of communication, it does not fit with the overall goal.

This group member is a '**lone wolf**'.

B   One of your group has agreed to carry out some work and has attended meetings and even joined in discussions. However, when it is time to show the group their ideas, they have a lot of excuses for why they have produced nothing at all.

This group member may be a '**free loader**' (but be careful, as there may be underlying reasons that are not due to laziness that mean they have failed to produce any work: it may be due to a lack of confidence, and perhaps they need more support and encouragement before they feel able to share).

C   Another member of your group has completed their assigned task with time to spare, and sends a group message to ask if anyone needs any help. They are supportive and encouraging to all the other members and willing to take on extra tasks, if necessary.

This group member is a '**facilitator**'.

Answer

C, a 'facilitator'.

ACTIVITY Self-reflection

Do you consider yourself a team player or a lone wolf (hopefully not a free loader!)?

....

....

What can you do to become a better team player?

....

....

Do you think some team members may lack confidence and need more support, both with doing their tasks and with presenting their work?

....

....

How can you help to build confidence for all team members?

....

....

A student told us →

'Although I am not lazy, I didn't feel confident that I could do the assigned task well enough, and that is why I didn't contribute very much. I think it is unfair to call me a free loader.'

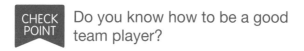

CHECK POINT Do you know how to be a good team player?

Why is being a team player an essential part of successful group working?

....

....

....

....

What characteristics does a great team player possess?

....

....

....

....

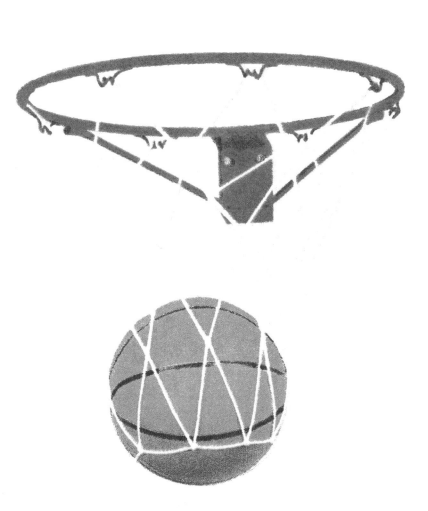

How do we make sure we work well as a group?

10 second summary

You will find out how to create and agree on a set of clear guidelines of what is expected of each group member, including shared obligations and responsibilities, and how this will minimise conflict.

Communication is key!

To make sure your group functions effectively and produces high quality
results, you need to establish and maintain effective communication.
This includes interpersonal and intercultural communication. Good
interpersonal communication involves being an effective speaker,
but perhaps more importantly being a good listener. Good speaking
involves being clear and to-the-point. Ideas should be focused and
clearly thought through. Good listening involves giving your team mates
the space and time to contribute to the group, and engaging with their
ideas. An effective team respects and trusts each other, and is prepared
to support and help throughout the project process.

'Most of my important lessons about life have come from recognizing how others from a different culture view things.'

Edgar H. Schein

Interpersonal communication

At the heart of any successful group is good **interpersonal communication**. This involves developing effective listening and speaking skills.

Interpersonal communication identifies and describes the ways people exchange information, emotions, and ideas through verbal (speaking and listening) and non-verbal (body language) messages via face-to-face engagement.

Top tips for being a good listener

- Consider and respect the speaker's ideas and feelings.

- Find ways to encourage your team mate to say more.

- Focus on the ideas and think of ways this could be valuable.

- Think of a question you could ask to develop the idea (when your team mate has finished talking).

- Link what they are saying to something you already know.

- Find at least one positive comment you could contribute to your team mate's idea.

- Try and avoid interruptions and respond when your team mate has finished.

Top tips for being a good speaker

- Prepare for your group meeting – write down some questions you'd like to ask.

- Aim to ask at least one question – with some evidence to support your point.

- Take your time, speak slowly and think about what you are saying.

- Make eye contact with your team mates – then they are more likely to engage with what you are saying.

- Be clear – try and stay focused on a single point. Don't waffle or digress.

- Be brief – keep it short. There's nothing more annoying than someone trying to dominate a conversation.

- Be ready to stop and allow others to speak – this shows that people are listening, and your idea may be developed further.

- Assert yourself, if necessary (without dominating the discussion or offending anyone).

- Summarise and repeat what you've said, so that everyone is clear.

Intercultural communication

At university, you are likely to be working in an international learning environment. Your group members might be from a variety of countries and cultures, and they may all have different ways of communicating. It is important to learn and understand these different communication norms in order to ensure effective communication and avoid misunderstandings.

One way to improve the **intercultural communication** of your group is to consider Hall's theory of **high- and low-context cultures** (1989), where direct and indirect communication are given different levels of importance and value.

The chart below highlights some of the typical characteristics associated with high- and low-context cultures.

Intercultural communication (sometimes called cross-cultural communication) the study of how different cultures and social groups communicate, behave and perceive the world around them, and how this might impact on groups and organisations that operate in an intercultural context.

High-context and low-context cultures a concept to describe how communication is given different levels of importance and value dependent on context.

High-context cultures	Low-context cultures
• Body language and facial expressions are important in the communication process – F2F is therefore preferred	• Verbal communication the most important way to communicate – F2F is less important
• Group identity and whole group decision making	• Individual identity – personal contributions and accomplishments are valued
• Getting it right is more important than finishing fast	• Targets and goals – linear progression is important
• Cooperation and stability of the group – discussion, argument and disagreements are avoided, dignity, honour and building 'face' are highly valued	• Problem solving via discussion and debate – emphasis on logic and reason, conflict is depersonalised
• Communal space – where preferred, physical distance between individuals is narrow	• Privacy and personal space – respectful distance is valued
• The whole picture may be required before an individual will contribute or the project can proceed	• Individuals will contribute to discussion with minimum knowledge
• Listeners will wait until the speaker has finished to respond, to allow due respect for the speaker's idea.	• Listeners may respond immediately and develop an idea in the course of the discussion. Interruption is common and acceptable.

Source: Based on Halverson, C.B. (2008) 'Social identity group and individual behaviour'. In *Effective multicultural teams: Theory and practice*. Dordrecht: Springer (pp. 43–79).

ACTIVITY Mapping high- and low-context cultures

Based on the characteristics highlighted above, cross where you would put yourself on the chart below:

Low Context   High Context

Hall's theory demonstrates how and why misunderstandings can occur in multicultural working groups. It is important, therefore, to take time to consider the multicultural dynamic of your group and factor in these different communication styles when working on your group task.

ACTIVITY   What do you know about different cultures?

Use the table above to begin a conversation in your group about how people from different cultures communicate with each other, and ask each other three questions:

- Do you agree or disagree with the list?

- Where do you sit on the context line?

- How can we avoid cultural misunderstandings?

By doing this you will discover some of these different cultural norms. And then you can work out how to incorporate them into your new group culture.

Tip!

It is important to bear in mind that this is a very simplistic representation of communication differences across the globe. There are of course many nuances, and individual behaviours can vary within different cultural and social contexts. For example, communication between friends and family will be different from communication and behaviour within a formal working group.

Cultures are also in a continuous state of change, and this needs to be factored in to any discussion you may have within your international group.

CHECK POINT Communication skills

What makes a good communicator and what could you do to improve your communication skills?

....

....

....

....

Congratulations

You have made sure your group is united, collaborative and working to achieve the same, shared goals. Now … you need to stay focused, meet deadlines and hand in a high quality project on time.

How do we keep on top of our project?

10 second summary

This section will show you how to unpack activities into achievable sub-tasks, the importance of regular meetings and how best to manage your time.

60 second summary

Meetings and milestones

The best way to keep on top of your project is to devise a development plan during the forming stage of group work. Your development plan should divide your project into manageable chunks of activity. It should include a progress timetable with achievable interim targets and who does what for each chunk, and scheduled regular meetings to check progress, update and troubleshoot any issues. Regular meetings are vital as they keep everyone on track and help to maintain group identity and unity. Your development plan should also include contingencies, should things go wrong, such as role switching, targeted support and any individual support that may be required. Your development plan will help you stay organised, stay focused and stay on target to completion.

Your project development plan

Once you have decided your **team roles**, you can start to develop your **project development plan** and timetable. Here is a simple plan that you can adapt to suit your own group needs.

Team role the position and/or activities assigned to each person in a group designed to streamline workloads, decision making, productivity and overall effectiveness of group performance.

Project development plan an outline and timetable of activities and deadlines to help a group complete a project.

You shouldn't watch the clock, but you should clock the time.

PROJECT DEVELOPMENT PLAN				
Project name:				
Group members:				
Assignment:		Submission date:		
Phase 1				
What?	Who?	When?	Due?	Problems/solutions
Phase 2				
What?	Who?	When?	Due?	Problems/solutions
Reflective summary				

The plan includes:

Project name: This may be the title provided by your tutor, or your own.

Group members: Listing members here ensures you have an accurate record.

Assignment: This might include a summary of the brief and the type of group work you have been asked to do (e.g. report or presentation).

Submission date: It is a good idea to note this at the top of your development plan, as it will act as a reminder and prompt!

Phase 1 and Phase 2: These sections are optional. They will help you divide up your project into manageable chunks of activity with attainable deadlines.

What? Here you list the specific task that is required (e.g. create PowerPoint slides).

Who? Here you add the group member or members directly involved in that specific task.

When? Include the due date for each specific task.

Problems/solutions: This is another optional column. Here you could make a note of any issues that arose for each task, and how you resolved them. This is useful if you have been asked by your tutor to keep a reflective diary of your progress.

Reflective summary: If your assignment requires you to include a reflective diary or summary of your project, then include this here. You should aim to keep an ongoing record of progress rather than try and remember it all at the end. Ask yourself questions such as:

- What went right and what went wrong, and why?
- What lessons have you learnt?
- What new skills have you acquired?
- What would you do differently next time?

A student told us

'I don't know what to do when I can't meet the group deadline.'

What do we do when we are falling behind schedule?

If you find that you are falling behind schedule because everything is taking longer than you thought it would, or because you have other work to do that has taken priority, you need to take action.

There are decisions you need to make as a group. With the remaining time, can you continue with the original plan, or do you need to make changes?

If you decide you need to make changes, these questions may help you decide what to do:

- Do you need to scale back what you are going to do? How much? How?

- Do you need to reorganise the team and change roles?

- Is there a role that is missing and now needs to be fulfilled?

- Are there any group members that are struggling? If so, how can you support them without taking their work away from them?

- Can you break the work up into more manageable chunks?

- Do you need to accept that the initial plan was too ambitious?

A student told us

'I am worried about what the group will think of my work – what if they think it is not very good?'

Remember, everyone will have some worries about what the rest of the group will think of their contribution. This is natural and normal.

There are some useful things you can do to make yourself feel better:

- Discuss your ideas and show your materials to someone you trust outside the group (and preferably outside the course) – if it's a presentation, practise your part with them.

- If you have created a 'ground rules agreement' (see Section 8), you should remind your group about it, and how it encourages respect for and support of each other.

- Try to look at your work through the eyes of the group. Does it do what it is meant to do? Is it going to fit with the other work being done?

- Assess your own view of its success or otherwise. Are you proud of it? If not, why not? Is there something you can do to help improve it?

- Finally, when you present your part of the group work to the group, ask them for advice and feedback and indicate your willingness to adapt or change – being defensive only causes conflict (see Section 7).

Strategies for keeping on top of your group work

ACTIVITY

Write a list of strategies that you will use to keep you on schedule and working as planned on your group project.

How I will stay on track

1 Strategy

....

....

2 Strategy

....

....

3 Strategy

....

....

4 Strategy

....

....

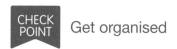

CHECK POINT Get organised

Have you tried these?

1 Have you created a project development plan? .... Yes / No

2 Do you know who is doing what? .... Yes / No

3 Are you aware of how much time you have to do
   your task(s)? .... Yes / No

4 Do you have strategies for dealing with any worries
   about your contribution? .... Yes / No

How do we avoid conflict?

10 second
summary

In this section, you will learn how to resolve common group working challenges and problems, such as dominant or reluctant group members, arguments and disagreements, illness or absence, and intercultural misunderstandings.

Set some guidelines

Misunderstandings, disagreements and conflict are probably the greatest
concern for most newly forming groups. The question of how to avoid,
reduce and/or remove conflict from your group can seem daunting.
However, one of the simplest and most effective methods of mitigating
worries and concerns is for your group to agree on an open and fair set
of group rules, which provide clear guidelines on what is expected of
each member. By agreeing, from the offset, on shared obligations and
expected behaviours, this can help to minimise future conflict, foster trust
and respect, anticipate possible issues and potential conflict scenarios,
and ensure every member contributes equally.

> Conflict can destroy a team which hasn't spent time learning to deal with it.

Establishing a group rules agreement

The best teams work in a conflict-free environment. While disagreement is part of the storming stage of any group, it can easily escalate into conflict, and that can be destructive for your group success. One of the easiest and most effective ways to reduce or eliminate conflict is for your group, from the outset, to agree on a fair set of group rules. These will provide clear guidelines on what is expected of each member and set out shared responsibilities. A **group rules agreement** is a contract of commitment; it can help to minimise conflict and ensure everyone is contributing equally to the task. It can also help you predict any future issues that may arise and how best to deal with them.

Group rules agreement
a document, agreed by the group, setting out expected behaviour during a group project, with the explicit purpose to prevent or reduce disagreement and conflict.

A student told us

'I don't know what to do if we don't get on well as a group.'

Here is a typical group rules agreement template that you can use:

Group rules agreement		
Group members:	**Signature:**	**Date:**
We, the above group members, agree to abide by the following ground rules:		
We agree to…		
1		
2		
3		
4		
5		

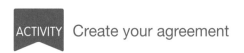

ACTIVITY Create your agreement

Use the following headings to put together a suitable agreement for your group (with some suggestions to get you started).

Group rules checklist
Shared goals **We will…** • *encourage a shared vision for our project*
Responsibilities **We will…** • *share tasks equally between us*
Behaviour **We will …** • *be respectful of others' views*
Participation **We will …** • *be pro-active, positive and work hard throughout the project*

Cooperation and collaboration

We will …

- *find positives during discussions and reach collective decisions*

Meetings

We will …

- *come prepared with all homework tasks complete*

Time management and deadlines

We will…

- *complete tasks on time*

Tip!

It is vital that every team member agrees to the group rules, and that you all follow them. You should therefore include guidelines on what to do if a member breaks the rules set by the group.

Working through possible points of conflict can help your group work out how to deal with them.

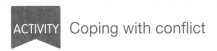

ACTIVITY Coping with conflict

What would you do to resolve the issue(s) in the following scenarios?

A: Two members have fallen out over a personal issue.

Resolution: ....

....

....

B: One member is dominating all discussions.

Resolution: ....

....

....

C: No one can agree on how to complete the project and time is being wasted.

Resolution: ....

....

....

D: One member is not contributing their share to the project.

Resolution: ....

....

....

E: The group seems to have split into two competing factions.

Resolution: ....

....

....

Can you think of any more?

A: If you have established group rules, then your chairperson or team leader could remind members not to bring personal issues to the group, and remind the group that everyone will suffer if the assignment is not handed in on time. The chair or a 'neutral' friend could also talk to the pair (together or separately) and ask them to either resolve or set aside their differences for the sake of the group. If the situation continues to escalate, you should consider talking to your tutor and asking for her/his advice.

B: Your appointed team leader/chair could politely remind the group that 'everyone' should have time to speak. If this doesn't work, the chair could (again politely) take the talkative member to one side and ask him/her to refrain from dominating the meetings.

C: You need to simplify your decision-making process. You could appoint (or change) a team leader to make final decisions and draw a line under debate and discussions. You need to act quickly and make bold and perhaps difficult decisions that will involve compromises across the group.

D: Your team leader or chair could remind 'everyone' of the importance of shared responsibilities and workloads. If his behaviour continues, perhaps a friend or the chair could have a private word with him. If the situation worsens, then the group could threaten to report his lack of commitment to the tutor, and you will request that he is removed from the group and the assignment grading.

E: The team leader or chair (in a position of neutrality) could identify positives in each camp, highlight common ground between the two factions and encourage collaboration rather than competition. And remind the group that the group mark is what counts.

Tip!

Nip it in the bud

If conflict does arise, in whatever form, it is important to deal with it quickly before it escalates further. Your group rules agreement can be used as a starting point for conflict resolution meetings.

CHECK POINT Consider how to resolve conflict

How do you feel about a group rules agreement? Can you foresee any issues with using one?

....

....

....

....

In what other ways might you reduce the risk of disagreement and conflict in your group?

....

....

....

....

What makes a great final product?

10 second
summary

This section will show you how to
draw together individual contributions
to create a single, high quality and
unified product.

60 second
summary

The finish line is in sight

The final and arguably most important part of your group project is the editing stage. Editing should be an activity that runs throughout your project, and should not be left to the last minute. You should make sure you timetable interim edits in your development plan so that the product is continuously improved. Your final edit or run-through, however, is your opportunity to make adjustments that can elevate your project to spectacular status. The editing process can be difficult and complex but, by appointing a skilled editor and then dividing editing tasks into discrete segments that focus on particular areas, you should be able to shape, hone and tweak your project until it is of a high standard.

> The first draft is monochrome, the second is sepia, the third lets the sunlight in and the fourth is in glorious technicolour.

Review, revise, reflect

Copyediting and **proofreading** are critical tasks, and your team need to make sure you allow plenty of time to make the necessary changes and improvements, and ensure successful completion and delivery of a quality group product.

Make sure that revision and editing are factored into your project development plan. They need to take place throughout the project and not left until the end. This makes editing your final draft much, much easier!

Copyediting a systematic process of examining the effectiveness of the content, structure, style and language used to communicate the purpose of the project to the reader or listener.

Proofreading the process of finding and correcting grammar, spelling and punctuation errors before a project is submitted. This is the final step in the editing process and takes place once the draft is complete.

How you review depends on a number of factors, including project type and how you have assigned roles. But review should be thorough and complete before you hand your assignment in.

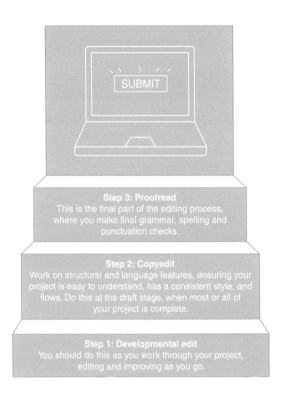

Step 3: Proofread
This is the final part of the editing process, where you make final grammar, spelling and punctuation checks.

Step 2: Copyedit
Work on structural and language features, ensuring your project is easy to understand, has a consistent style, and flows. Do this at the draft stage, when most or all of your project is complete.

Step 1: Developmental edit
You should do this as you work through your project, editing and improving as you go.

You could assign one editor or more to complete each stage of the editing process.

Developmental editing
a form of scrutinisation of documents with the purpose of troubleshooting issues, continuously improving quality and ensuring the project stays on track.

A student told us

'Editing is so tedious. How can I stop my brain switching off?'

Editing procedure

Here is a handy guide to help you develop an effective editing procedure:

- Allow plenty of time for multiple edits and final proofread.

- Edit in short, intense bursts and let your edit rest before you return to it.

- Divide editing and proofreading into discrete topic areas and focus on each of those one at a time. As you read, ask the following questions:

Content

Does our project address the task throughout?

Is everything relevant?

Do all our citations relate directly to the project topic and our aim?

Is our purpose and/or line of argument clear?

Have we missed anything?

Is it the right length?

Research material

Have we included sufficient examples and evidence to support the points we make?

Are our ideas expressed logically and clearly?

Have we used sources effectively?

Have we analysed and evaluated the strengths, weaknesses and reliability of our sources?

Structure

Do our ideas link together and does our project flow?

Is each paragraph well structured?

Have we presented information in the right order?

Is it clear how one paragraph leads to the other?

Does it make sense when we read it out loud?

Style

Have we used the correct style throughout?

Is it too chatty?

Have we used technical vocabulary clearly and accurately?

Are the words we use our own, except for quotations (no plagiarism!)?

Clarity

Is there anything the reader will find confusing?

Is our use of language clear and accessible?

Is our line of reasoning/argument logical and easy to follow?

Are our sentences a reasonable length and uncomplicated? (Can I read them out loud without running out of oxygen?)

General

Does our introduction grab the reader/listener's attention?

Does the conclusion provide an effective recap and interesting sign-off?

Is our spelling, grammar and punctuation all correct?

Is our referencing accurate?

Is our reference list correct and complete?

Presentation projects: practice makes perfect

Make sure you allow plenty of time to practise your presentation project together.

Check for:

- Running order and transitions

- Timings and flow

- Visuals/use of technology

Tip!

Try recording your presentation on your phone. It is likely the recording will reveal issues about your presentation that you might have missed, such as speed and clarity of your articulation, clumsy transitions, poor body language, lack of eye contact, and so on.

ACTIVITY Typical editing problems

How would you solve the following editing issues?

Write down your solutions below.

Our project is too short, what can we do?

....

....

....

Our project is too long, what can we do?

....

....

....

We can't find relevant sources to support our project, what can we do?

....

....

....

The structure of our project is all over the place and the style is inconsistent. What can we do?

....

....

....

The C-list

Before you *finally* submit your group project, run through our **C**-list to check the quality of your work.

Clear

Is every part of your project clear and easy to follow? Have a clear focus and purpose been identified?

Concise

Are ideas succinct, to the point and incisive? Is there any waffle?

Cohesive

Does the work flow and do ideas link together? Does the project develop with a clear sense of direction and purpose?

Consistent

Is the style consistent throughout? Does the project look like a team effort with one unified voice?

Collaborative

Has everyone contributed equally? If not, why not?

Constructive

Does the project build a solid, interesting and informed response to the task, with significant and useful outcomes?

Creative

Does your project demonstrate a creative and original approach to the task? Does it present new interpretations of old ideas, and innovative approaches and solutions to the issues?

CHECK POINT Post-project reflections

Once you have completed and submitted your project, take some time to think about how things went. Consider the following questions:

- What went well and less well? Why?

- Is there anything you would do differently?

- What new skills have you learnt?

- What lessons will you feed forward into your next group working project?

- Have your feelings changed about group working? For better or worse?

Final checklist: How well did you do?

Tick all the points you covered during your group working project:

We got to know each other (strengths, concerns, likes, dislikes) ☐

We got to know the task ☐

We devised a group rules agreement ☐

We assigned roles and tasks ☐

We created a plan and a timetable ☐

We set achievable interim deadlines ☐

We arranged regular face-to-face meetings ☐

We predicted potential problems (and dealt with them effectively) ☐

We met targets and stayed on track ☐

We edited our work until it was fit for submission ☐

We submitted our group project on time ☐

Glossary

Conflict   a negative interpersonal issue that occurs between two or more members of a team, that may adversely affect performance of the whole group, and the quality of the project.

Copyediting   a systematic process of examining the effectiveness of the content, structure, style and language used to communicate the purpose of the project to the reader or listener. Copyediting is more detailed than developmental editing.

Developmental editing   a form of scrutinisation of documents during a project with the purpose of troubleshooting issues, continuously improving quality and ensuring the project stays on track. A developmental edit may focus on content, structure, continuity and flow.

Diversity   the different types of people that may make up groups (in terms of nationality, race, religion, gender, age, disability, etc.).

Employability   the attributes of a person that enable them to gain and maintain employment.

Group development theory (Forming, Storming, Norming, Performing)
Bruce Tuckman's theory sets out the process a group goes through when it works on a task, from the initial formation stage, through facing

challenges, dealing with and solving problems, to finally working effectively to complete the project.

Group rules agreement   a document, agreed by the group, setting out the expected behaviour during a group project, with the explicit purpose to prevent or reduce disagreement and conflict.

High-context and low-context cultures   a concept to describe how communication is given different levels of importance and value. For example, in the high-context cultures of Asia, Africa and the Middle East, there is an emphasis on trust and collective decision making; whereas in low-context cultures, greater value is placed on individuality and process-led decision making.

Inclusivity   the practice or policy of including many different types of people, who may otherwise be excluded, and treating them with fairness and equity.

Intercultural communication (sometimes called cross-cultural communication) the study of how different cultures and social groups communicate, behave and perceive the world around them, and how this might impact on groups and organisations that operate in an intercultural context.

Interpersonal communication identifies and describes the ways people exchange information, emotions, and ideas through verbal (speaking and listening) and non-verbal (body language) messages via face-to-face engagement.

Project development plan an outline and timetable of activities and deadlines to help a group complete a project.

Proofreading the process of finding and correcting grammar, spelling and punctuation errors before a project is submitted. This is the final step in the editing process and takes place once the draft is complete.

Reflection a process of thinking deeply about past activities, feelings and behaviours in order to develop skills and enhance future performance.

Scenario a story that describes and speculates on possible actions or events in the future.

Team player a group member who puts what's good for their group before their own personal preferences. A good team player acts to ensure the success of their group.

Team role the position and / or activities assigned to each person in a group designed to streamline workloads, decision making, productivity and overall effectiveness of group performance.

Time management the process of organising and using time effectively to improve productivity.

Further reading and resources

Hall, E.T. (1989) *Beyond Culture*. Norwell, MA: Anchor Press.

Ground-breaking work by anthropologist Edward Hall that sets out to explain how different cultures communicate.

Hopkins, D. and Reid, T. (2018) *The Academic Skills Handbook: Your Guide to Success in Writing, Thinking and Communicating at University*. London: Sage.

Our all-in-one Academic Skills toolkit includes an extended chapter on group working, with further guidance, tips and tasks.

Lencioni, P. (2006) *Overcoming the Five Dysfunctions of a Team*. Hoboken, NJ: John Wiley & Sons.

Lencioni's complementary book walks you through essential strategies to fix your team.

Lencioni, P.M. (2012) *The Five Dysfunctions of a Team: Team assessment*. USA, NJ: John Wiley & Sons.

An entertaining and invaluable guide to what not to do when working in teams.

Tuckman, B.W. and Jensen, M.A.C. (1977) 'Stages of small-group development revisited', *Group & Organization Studies*, 2(4): 419–427.

Provides further detail of and some interesting revisions to Tuckman's group development theory.